Recipes & Rascals

Food and Funny Goings-on in *Yorkshire*

Sue Hiscoe

Dock Pudding

by Fay Blackburn

May teases out your pale green lips
As you lie nurtured in your *Calder bed*
Gently seducing your most tender tips
For nettle, alum and oat to wed

And when in *gastronomic bliss* you lie
Upon my soft white breakfast plate
partnered with such sweet bacon fried
Polygonium Bistorta consummate

Goings-on

When Nick, Sophie *(Springer Spaniel)* and I became 'incomers' to what we ashamedly and secretly then called *Cleckhuddersfax*, we were greeted with such a warm welcome.

We had no cooking facilities in our house to start with and on the night we moved in we resorted to take-away pizza when feeding our helpers Graham and Craig.

On the second night, we thought we should search for something better and Nick announced that he was going to turn left at the end of the road to see what happened. I thought he'd disappear into the dark abyss of *Lancashire border moorland*, never to be seen again!

Across the bridge he saw a glow that turned out to be *The Brown Cow Inn*. He waded through the revellers and found the Landlord and Landlady, Kevin and Christine Parker.

"Is it possible to have anything to eat?" Nick asked.

Kevin replied, *"You can have anything you want, anytime you want and what took you so long ..... Nick?"*

The party began that night and now, over a decade later, the people of this valley continue to show us the warmest friendship and the greatest kindness imaginable *(while also introducing us to some decidedly strange goings-on!)*

This book is dedicated to all our friends. xxx

Recipes

The World Dock Pudding Championships

Mytholmroyd is where the poet *Ted Hughes* was born and not far from Heptonstall, where his wife *Sylvia Plath* is buried.

The *Dock Pudding Championships* are held here each Spring and the tasting panel are helped in their deliberations by the *Hebden Bridge Junior Brass Band*.

If you visit the Championships this year, look out for *Doris Hirst of Cragg Road*. She's a true devotee and multiple world champion, and she always sits just on the left as you walk through the entrance door of the *Mytholmroyd* Leisure and Community Centre. Ask her nicely and she'll let you taste her award-winning pudding.

The pudding itself

Dock Pudding is made from dock leaves, nettles, oatmeal (to bulk it out), any available alums (onions, spring onions, but never garlic*), butter and seasoning.

It goes back to the *19th century,* when poverty was high and a lot of people had scurvy by February, thanks to the winter diet of salt pork, beans and bread.

Dock leaves and nettles were the first spring greens to appear after the winter stores had run out and before the new season's vegetables were ready.

The dock leaf used in pudding isn't the common cow dock leaf (the one we used to put on nettle stings when younger), but a sweet variety called *Bistort or Passion dock* – so called because it appears around *Passiontide.*

The taste is like a cross between spinach and asparagus and it's said to form part of a traditional Yorkshire breakfast.

Unaware of its delicate flavour, the second world war German propagandist *William Joyce (Lord Haw Haw)* announced on radio that food rationing was so bad in England that Yorkshire people were reduced to eating grass!

The Dock Pudding recipe has many closely guarded family variations and people have been known to freeze a freshly made spring pudding and have it for breakfast on Christmas morning!

* One year, someone added garlic to their pudding recipe. Naturally, it caused an outcry and immediate disqualification.

13

Dock Pudding

Contributed by Fay Blackburn

Wash **2lb fresh young dock leaves** and **½lb young nettle tops**. Peel and finely chop **2 large onions**. Boil all three together in a little salted water until the onions are tender. Add **2 or 3 tablespoons of oatmeal** and simmer for a further 20 mins stirring frequently.

Strain off the excess liquid, add a **knob of butter** in to the mix and adjust seasoning if necessary. This may be put in a jar and kept until required or can be deep frozen.

To use – take a large spoonful of the pudding and fry in melted bacon fat (important, – but if vegetarian olive oil would be fine).

For a traditional Yorkshire breakfast serve with fried bacon and eggs.

Fay Blackburn is a former committee member of the *World Dock Pudding competition* and for many years compered the proceedings. Fay lives in *Erringden,* she tells me that the Bistort can be easily found behind the Community and Leisure Centre in Mytholmroyd.

Nancy Smith (a very good family friend) who with her granddaughter *Megan Masters* made the Dock Pudding opposite (they came third in the 2010 World Dock Pudding Championship) tells me that the Royal Horticultural Society have started to supply *Polygonum Bistorta* for its delightful pink flower and pretty foliage.

Many thanks to Richard of Heptonstall Museum who kindly showed me his secret place for the shot on the previous page.

Nettle Soup

*with Bistort Dock Leaves (optional) or watercress or cos lettuce
or any other wild greens*

Ingredients

**1 carrier bag full of nettle tops
or young leaves**

2 tbsps oil

2 large onions sliced finely

2 large carrots, sliced

4 celery stalks, chopped

2 large garlic cloves, smashed

2 litres vegetable stock

½ tsp grated nutmeg

**6 tbsps cooked brown rice
(or med potato)**

2 tbsps frozen peas

Chives or parsley garnish

Black pepper and salt to taste

Wash the nettle tops thoroughly. Tougher stalks should be removed (if you use rubber gloves you won't get stung!). Heat the oil in a a large saucepan and sweat the onion, garlic, carrots and celery.

When softened add the stock and the leaves. Bring to the boil and simmer until the leaves are tender. Throw in the frozen peas till cooked. Remove from the heat.

Add the nutmeg and season. Add the cooked rice (or cooked potato, diced) and liquidise.

If serving hot, return to the heat checking the seasoning. Garnish with chopped herbs of your choice.

This does sound weird, but is truly delicious it tastes like a cross between asparagus and watercress, is just as scrumptious cold too. It is very very nutritious, full of vitamins and minerals, a great blood cleanser.

Spear Pie

This is eaten in memory a of young *Yorkshire lad* who played an important part in the fighting at *Stamford Bridge* against the Danes on *September 25th 1066.* (7 roman miles from York).

The Derwent River at that site was crossed by a wooden bridge held by a *Danish soldier* to prevent the English from reaching the left bank of the river. Forty soldiers had fought against him but each had been slain by his axe. However, this *canny Yorkshire lad* had a bright idea and on finding a tub usually used for feeding the pigs he got into it and floated downstream until he was directly under the soldier standing on the bridge. Using his long spear and aiming very carefully he dislodged the enemy and so allowed the English soldiers access to the bridge and the left bank.

For hundred of years, until 1878 this victory and the bravery of the Yorkshire lad were celebrated each year on the *first Sunday after September 19th* and this was called *Spear Pie Feast* and afterwards the pie was only baked occasionally.

The pies were said to be made from raised pastry, boat shaped and filled with the kind of pear that was hard and late in ripening. They had a skewer sticking through the centre to call to mind the spear the lad used, but people unaware of the story and because they were filled with pears called them *Pear Pies*.

One pie, baked from the above, on *September 1966* at the *Feast at Stamford Bridge* (the 900th Anniversary of the battle) won the Silver Cup as a winner of the Pie competition.

Spear Pie with Raspberry Coulis

Ingredients

4 conference pears

Shortcrust pastry

Fine brown sugar

12 raspberries

1 tsp vanilla essence

Beaten egg

Soak raspberries in the vanilla essence. Pre heat oven to 170°C/325°F/Gas 3.

Chop the bottom of the pears to make an even flat base. Core the centre of the pears, and take out seeds. Peel the pears, leaving the stalk intact. Stuff the middle of the pears with the raspberries.

Roll out the pastry and cut into 1inch strips. Carefully press the pastry strip starting from the stalk, Roll round the pastry diagonally. Until you reach the base of the pear. Press together any tears, and coat with the beaten egg.

Sprinkle with the brown sugar and bake for 25–35 minutes until golden brown.

Serve on a bed of Raspberry Coulis and Brown Bread Ice Cream. Recipe on next page.

Raspberry Coulis

300g raspberries

2 tbsps caster sugar

Juice of 1 lemon

Mix together all ingredients, liquidize and press through a sieve.

Recipe and food styling
Michelle Wardingley

This may sound strange – but it is the most delicious ice cream ever!

22

Brown Bread Ice Cream

Serves 4

Ingredients

50g/2oz fresh wholemeal breadcrumbs

2 large eggs, separated

75g/3oz light soft brown sugar *

150ml/¼ pint double cream whipped in to soft peaks

1 tbsp coffee and chicory essences, or dark rum

* Soft brown sugar or golden sugar gives a lovely pale coffee colour, but caster sugar can be used for a whiter ice cream.

Mix the breadcrumbs and one third of the sugar together and spread over the base of a small baking tray and toast under a hot grill for about 5 mins turning occasionally, until golden and crunchy. Turn the crunchy crumbs on a plate and when completely cool crush coarsely with the back of a wooden spoon. Beat the egg yolks well and set aside.

In a large bowl whisk the egg whites until stiff. Whisk in the rest of the brown sugar a tablespoon at a time.

Using a large metal spoon fold in the egg yolks, whipped cream, crushed breadcrumbs and coffee and chicory.

Turn the mixture in to a 1-litre/2 pint metal container and cover securely with foil.

Freeze for 2 hours stirring lightly every 30 mins (to ensure that the breadcrumbs do not sink to the bottom). Leave for a further 2 hours, or until firm.

Before serving allow the ice cream to stand for 5 minutes to soften slightly.

Gaelic, Norse, it's all Yorkshire to me

Much of the present *West Riding of Yorkshire* was once part of the last Celtic Kingdom in England – *The Kingdom of Elmet.*

Our version of the *Gaelic language* was spoken here up to the *early 600's AD*. Something our Scottish cousins forget, is that the area up to and beyond Edinburgh was already English-speaking in the 300's AD.
So much for who is or isn't Celtic!

By the time *Elmet* was absorbed into the "English" Kingdom of Northumbria, the *Vikings* were already raiding and settling, so it's likely that our language moved from Gaelic into Norse influence. The word Riding itself comes from the Norse "*Thridding*" or third. It could well be, that the West Riding only came to English around the Norman invasion.

It's certainly a fact that a good part of the North was laid waste by the Normans as reprisals for non-cooperation (who would have thought that of a Yorkshireman?) Perhaps those who stole the land after that were English speakers.

Gervase Phinn, the broadcaster and humorist, himself a great *Yorkshireman*, tells a story about the language of the region. He was showing two Norwegian friends around England. They had very good English and only struggled with the strongest of regional accents. They had made their way to Yorkshire and were in a pub talking to a couple of locals. *"Wheer's tha banna lig a'neet?"* said one (where are you going to stay tonight?). Before *Gervase* could provide a translation, one of his companions answered that they had found rooms in the local hotel. "How did you make sense of that?" asked Gervase. *"Because he spoke Old Norse",* came the answer.

by Duncan Newsome

The Pork Pie Appreciation Society Ripponden

In 1982 a health club opened in *Ripponden*. Some of the men who joined also liked a pint, so they thought it perfectly reasonable to replace the calories used in their Saturday workout with beer at the nearby *Bridge Inn*.

Much to the envy of the others, one of the regulars brought a *pork pie* to eat while drinking, so another member of the group offered to start bringing enough pies for everyone every week as he knew where to get some really good ones.

A few months later, *Bob (the pie fetcher)* was unable fulfil his commitment so it was then decided that his role of pie-fetcher should be shared, so they took it in turns to choose and bring the pies in a *wooden tea box*.

Inevitably, comparisons were made and *marks began to be awarded* these were written on the tea box along with a current event or a sporting event (the quirkier the better).

As the months and years went by, this informal group became a Society, and then a global authority on the appearance, texture and taste of pork pies.

Pie makers from all over the country covet their praise and compete for their accolades, and on the night that the clocks 'go forward ' usually the *last Saturday in March*, the Society holds a contest for Britain's butchers and bakers that now attracts over *50 entrants*.

At Christmas, the president of the Society awards prizes. There is *Pie Fetcher of the Year* (the member with the highest average of marks over the year), *The Farthest Fetch, Most Expensive Pie, Cheapest Pie, Highest Attendance over the Year,* and finally *The Wooden Spoon Award* for the lowest average marks over the year. This particular wooden spoon is actually 3 feet long and more of a shovel than a spoon!

My pork pie recipe has the approval of the Society, though the pastry is different to that made by most butchers and you'll find the taste and texture are different to a shop-bought pie.

When you've made it, you and your family might like to follow the Society's recommended judging process:

Pies should be eaten in relative quiet. Comments that may influence others in subsequent marking are frowned upon.

Have at hand a condiments box, containing a wide range of sauces, pickles and mustards.

If no one reaches for any of them, the pie is good. If Soy Sauce, Worcester Sauce or Tabasco are required, there is clearly a problem.

Once the pie has been eaten, each judge must write down a mark out of ten on a card, without conferring. Then you must each explain to the others what you think of the pie – its look, taste and texture – in detail.

The pie fetcher (the cook in our case) is allowed to be biased, but not by more than two points over the average!

Pork Pie

Ingredients

1lb fresh lean pork

1lb flour

3oz fat

2 sage leaves and seasoning

Pinch of salt

½ tsp baking powder

½ pint stock ⎫
1oz gelatine ⎭ optional

Egg and milk for glaze

Cut the pork into a small dice and place on a plate with 2 tablespoons of water. Add the sage and seasoning and let them soak well.

Rub the fat into the flour until it resembles fine breadcrumbs, add the baking powder with the salt and mix with water to a stiff paste.

Thinly roll out the pastry and line a medium greased pie/cake tin with it. Cut the pastry neatly off 1 inch above the edge and roll out this part to form a lid.

Fill the tin with the pork etc, moisten the edges and put the lid on, pressing the edges well together.

Cut a large hole in the centre, brush with egg and milk and bake in a good oven for 2 hours.

Make ½ pint stock with the trimmings, add the gelatine dissolved in water, and strain this through the hole whilst the pie is still hot, then leave till cool.

In years gone by the hole in the centre of the pie was created by the pork butcher sticking his little finger in to the pastry!

To make your own jelly:

Put **1 pigs foot** in a stew pan and cover with **water**, and simmer until the meat drops from the bones. Then take out the meat and pour the liquid in the pie and let it stand overnight.

Onion Marmalade

From the early 1900's

Good served with sausage and mash, particularly in the winter.

Take a large frying pan and heat **2 tablespoons of olive oil** with a small amount of **sea salt and pepper**. Add **2¼ lbs onions** (peeled and finely chopped). Cook over a medium heat for about ¼ hour until the onions start to soften but not brown, stirring occasionally.

Turn the heat up a little more and add **one small glass of red wine** plus **3 fl ozs balsamic vinegar**. Stir until all is combined. Cook for a few minutes then lower the heat again, add **6 tablespoons of dark brown sugar** and stir well.

Leave to simmer on a low heat for about ¾ of an hour, stirring occasionally, until all the liquid has nearly evaporated. After checking the seasoning, pour in to sterilized jars and leave to cool.

Keep for a few days before using so that the flavour can develop.

I asked my very good friend and restaurateur Hansa (Leeds) how, in your Gujarati restaurant, on earth do you cope with all the peeling and chopping of onions and Hansa gave me a top tip: put your whole onions in the freezer for 20 minutes before you need to prepare them. I can't tell you how grateful I am to her, it does really really work!

Green Tomato Chutney

This proves to be very useful when your tomatoes don't ripen!

Ingredients

6lb green tomatoes

3lb carrots

2lb cooking apples

1 quart of vinegar

3lb demerara sugar

1 tsp ground mace

12 cloves

1½ tsp white pepper

4oz mustard seed

1½ tsp cayenne pepper

4oz salt

1 bay leaf

Red pepper (optional for colour)

Chop the apples and tomatoes into pieces with the sliced onions and cook in the vinegar for 1 hour.

Add the sugar, bruised cloves, mace, pepper, mustard seed, salt and bay leaf and, if using, the red pepper finely chopped, and cook for a further 1½hours. Put in warmed sterilized jars and seal airtight.

If you need to bulk it out any courgettes and marrows are useful additions.

31

Broad Bean, Goats Cheese & Tomato Tartlet

Makes six small tartlets or one 10-inch tart

Ingredients

12oz/335g shortcrust pastry

4 extra large eggs

½oz/12g butter

7floz/200ml double cream

2oz parmesan cheese grated

Freshly ground black pepper

**2 tbsps onion marmalade
- recipe previous page**

15 teeny cherry tomatoes halved

2 tbsps fresh/frozen broad beans

Basil leaves

Line the greased pastry tin with the rolled out shortcrust pastry, making sure that it is even on the base and sides and that there are no holes. Prick with a fork and refrigerate for 30 minutes.

Meanwhile cook the broad beans in boiling water for 5 minutes. Remove and run the beans under a cold tap to cool then slip off the grey outer skins. Put the beans to one side.

When the pastry case has been chilled, line with parchment paper or baking foil and fill with baking beans and bake at 375°C/190°F/Gas 5 for 20 minutes. Carefully remove the foil and baking beans and leave until completely cold.

Pour into a large mixing bowl the cream, 2 whole eggs and 2 egg yolks, the butter and the parmesan season and mix well.

Spread the pastry base with the onion marmalade and pour in the egg mixture. Gently arrange the tomato halves on top. Cover with foil bake for 20 minutes. When the egg mixture has set quickly take the tart from the oven and gently scatter the broad beans and torn goats cheese on top and return to the oven for a few minutes.

Drop on some basil leaves, grind some black pepper and serve warm with new potatoes and rocket salad.

Wensleydale Chicken Kiev with Ham & Leek Sauce

Serves 4

Ingredients

4 skinless chicken breasts

4oz real Wensleydale cheese

1 egg beaten

Plain flour for coating

4oz fresh brown bread crumbs grated

2 large leeks

2oz ham cut into small chunks

2 tbsps sunflower oil

White sauce

Cut a slit in the side of the chicken, to make a pocket.

Crumble the cheese and place in the pocket.

Coat the chicken carefully with the flour, egg and then cover with the breadcrumbs. Loosely wrap baking foil around the chicken breasts. Place in the oven in an oven-proof dish.

Bake for 30 – 40 minutes in a moderate oven until the chicken is cooked through.

Meanwhile, chop and fry the leeks in a pan, until soft. Add the ham chunks. Mix together with the white sauce.

Unwrap the baking foil and return the chicken to the oven until the breadcrumbs are toasty and the Wensleydale has melted.

Serve with the sauce poured over the chicken and with new potatoes

To be absolutely correct, the name Kiev should only be used when there is garlic in the recipe!

Beef & Black Sheep Pie

Serves 2

Ingredients

700g beef chopped into chunks

1 red onion

3 tbsps sunflower oil

2 cloves garlic

250ml Black Sheep Ale

250ml beef stock

25g plain flour

250g puff pastry

Thyme

1 egg beaten

2 tbsps of milk

Dust beef chunks with flour and fry in the oil till sealed or brown. Set aside.

Fry onion and garlic till soft. Return beef to pan add, beef stock, thyme and ale. Mix together and cook for a few minutes.
Pour into oven dish and bake in oven on 180°C/350°F/Gas 4 for 50-60 minutes.

Take out of the oven, give it a stir.

Roll out pastry. Brush the sides of the dish with the egg and place pastry over the meat, cut away excess pinch the sides together cut a couple of slits in the middle of the pie. Mix the rest of the milk and egg together, and brush the top of the pie.

Return to the oven for a further 20 minutes or until the pastry is golden brown.

Serve with Horseradish mash

The Rascals of Burnt Platts

In *1790*, on *Pole Moor, Scammonden* there was a place of ill repute. It was part of the *Duke of Leeds'* estate and was called *'Burnt Platts'*

The inhabitants were a party of travelling people called *Doudies* and the story goes that they were literally savage. No man would go near them alone and many a parent would threaten their naughty child with a trip to see the *Burntplatters!*

They built huts from stray stones and thatched the roofs with sods of grass.

They took no notice of rules or regulations and had their own wild laws and a kind of government.

They lived by *hunting,* making *whisky* and *weaving.* It was said that they owned but one knife for the whole community and they would pass this through the inner walls of their houses to one another.

They cooked in the open, on hot stones over a wood fire and made, among other things, a cross between a scone and a rock cake which became known as a *Rascal*.

The *Burntplatters* lived for so many years on the land, paying no rent or rates, that they could have claimed permanent possession, but one clever bailiff persuaded them to pay a shilling a year.

This changed their status and enabled the authorities to evict them.

So called as they used to be cooked on a bake stone or a griddle over a peal or turf fire in the villages above the moors in North Riding in Elizabethan times. Is a cross between a rock cake and a scone.

40

Turf Cakes or Fat Rascals

Ingredients

50g/2oz lard

50g/2oz butter

150ml/5floz whipping cream, slightly soured

350g/12oz plain flour

25g/1oz candied mixed peel

75g/3oz caster sugar (golden)

1 heaped tsp baking powder

75g/3oz currants

Rub the fat into the flour, add all the dry ingredients and then mix to a stiff paste with the cream.

Roll out to 2cm/¾ inch thickness and then cut into 10 to 12 rounds. Decorate if you wish with candied fruit/cherries/almonds.

Place on baking sheet and bake at 220°C/425°F/Gas 7 for 10 to 15 mins.

Ready to eat when cooled

Fat Rascals

Ingredients

150g each of plain flour and self raising flour

1 tsp baking powder

150g dried mixed fruit

1 medium egg yolk

150 g butter

50ml milk

100g caster sugar

1 tsp cinnamon powder

½ tsp grated nutmeg

Grated zest of each of a lemon and orange

1 medium egg yolk

1 tbsp water

Pinch of salt

Blanched whole almonds and glacé cherries to decorate

Rub the butter in to the sieved flours and baking powder. Add the mixed dried fruit, sugar, spices, orange and lemon zests. Lightly beat the egg and add with enough milk to make the mixture into a dough consistency. Divide in to 8 and pat into 2 cm deep rounds.

Mix egg yolk, salt and water together and glaze each rascal. Finish with the whole almonds and glacé cherries.

Bake until golden brown for about 15-20 minutes at 200°C/Gas 6

West Riding Soggy Moggy

– well it's a lighter and moister version of Yorkshire Parkin

Ingredients

10oz/275g self raising flour

2 eggs

4 tbsps treacle

4oz/110g sugar

4oz/110g lard and margarine mixed

A pinch of salt

2 tsps of fresh ginger – fresh ginger rather than ground, and 2 tablespoons for a more gingery taste.

Warm the fat and treacle until thin, mix with dry ingredients and add beaten eggs, pour into a greased tin (8inx12in) bake in a fairly moderate oven, 170°C/325°F/Gas 3/ for 30 or 40 minutes or until firm to the touch.

The Krumlin Pop Festival

Like most parts of the UK, *Halifax* had a thriving folk club scene in the late 60's.

Brian Highley and *Derek McEwan* were young local promoters who planned a modest folk festival, until a large tract of land at *Krumlin* was offered and their ambitions expanded somewhat.

Extreme self-confidence and a genius for persuasion led to the grandly named *Yorkshire Folk, Blues & Jazz Festival,* which was to take place at *Banquet House Farm in August 1970.*

Up to 50,000 people were expected between Friday night and Sunday afternoon and the line-up was to die for – *Elton John, Yes, The Who, Alan Price, Pink Floyd* and *Zoot Money* were all slated to appear.

Although the weather didn't co-operate, the event began well, with *20,000* arriving at the start of the weekend, *15,000* of whom were camping overnight.

Friday's shows were great and Saturday really rocked, but by Saturday night, there was trouble.

A fierce storm blew in and the temperature dropped to almost freezing. Most tents were completely blown away, *the stage, beer tent and other festival structures all collapsed and 70 people had to be hospitalised.* Over *330 cases of exposure* were treated on the site, though thankfully, there were no fatalities.

The event was abandoned on Sunday morning with the site (and the festival's finances) in a complete shambles.

The organisers later appeared at Halifax Bankruptcy Court, owing £30,796.

...and the refreshments?

There was a milk tent (yes, milk) and a *Tetley beer tent,* whose stock went walkabout when the tent blew down – though it was one of the last to go.

The souvenir brochure boasts about the scale of the catering:

50 tons firewood for camp fires, 2 1/2 tons sausages, 3 tons hamburgers, 6 tons chicken, 2 tons steak, 10,000 tins beans, 20 tons potatoes, 100,000 bread rolls, 10,000 loaves, 10,000 gallons soup, crisps to reach the top of mount Everest, 10,000 pints ice cream, 12,000 gallons beer, 50,000 sandwiches, 10,000 packets pop corn, 100,000 pints milk and 100,000 cans mineral water.

There's some doubt about the veracity of those claims, however. The civil aid report for the festival shows that they provisioned just 5,000 portions of bread and soup!

Just think – if it hadn't been for the local weather, *Krumlin* might have entered the English popular vocabulary instead of *Glastonbury!*

Ian and Jeanette Harkness the present owners of *Banquet House Farm* held a little 40th anniversary tribute event in August 2010 for invited guests only. The weather wasn't much better than the first time around, but the pies were great and *Zoot Money* agreed to come and play again, rocking the place into the small hours!

Root Vegetable Crisps

Use any root vegetables you have or desire but the below is a lovely mix

Ingredients

1 parsnip

1 carrot

1 celeriac

2-3 beetroots

2 golden sweet potatoes

Veg oil for deep frying such as rapeseed oil or safflower oil

Sea salt for sprinkling

Peel and slice the veg as thin as you can – the thinner you slice the crispier they will be.. If you're not an expert with a knife you can use the slicer disc on a food processor or a Japanese slicing mandolin or even a broad swivel peeler. To make the crisps – heat the oil in a deep fat fryer to 180°C. Fry the sliced vegetables in batches a couple of minutes each.

Drain on kitchen paper, sprinkle with salt and set aside. (You may or may not need to crisp in oven before serving)

*Roasted Vine Tomato Consommé and
Butternut Squash Soup recipes on next page*

Fresh Pea Soup

*best served as a chilled soup it the summer, but still vibrant
and flavoursome warmed*

Ingredients

25g butter

300g floury potatoes, cubed

**Bunch of spring onions finely
sliced**

850ml vegetable stock

**900g Peas in their pods, podded
or**

200g fresh or frozen peas

200g natural Greek yoghurt

Fresh chives snipped

Add the potatoes to the melted
butter in a pan and stir well. Cover
and cook gently for 5 mins. Add
the spring onions and the stock
and bring to the boil. Cover and
cook until the potatoes are just
tender – about 10 mins. Add the
peas and cook for 3 mins, Puree
the soup in a liquidiser or blender.
Pour in to a bowl and whisk in the
Greek yoghurt and leave to cool.
When cool cover and allow to chill
in the fridge.

Serve with the chives

Roasted Vine Tomato Consommé

The vine tomatoes give this soup a lovely intense flavour as well as a wonderful colour

Ingredients

650g/1½lb ripe vine tomatoes, halved

Salt and pepper

2 tbsps olive oil

1 onion peeled and chopped

1 large carrot, scrubbed and chopped

1 whole red chilli

1 tsp paprika

850ml/1½ pints chick or veg stock

1 tbsp fresh Basil finely shredded

Coat the tomatoes with ½ the olive oil and roast at Gas 5/375°F/90°C for 45 minutes.

When nearing the end of cooking time, in a large saucepan fry the onions, chilli and carrot in the tablespoonful of olive oil that remains. Stir in the paprika, add the roasted tomatoes and pour over the stock. Bring to the boil and with the lid half on simmer for 15 mins. Strain the tomatoes through a sieve over a large bowl to allow the juices to pass through. The veg should not be forced through. Discard the veg when drained. Return the soup to the pan, reheat and season. Sprinkle with torn basil.

Serves 4

Butternut Soup

Slice an **onion** and soften in a pan with **1 tbsp in butter or oil**. Add cubed **med/lge butternut squash**. Add **850 ml/1½ pints chicken** or vegetable stock and simmer until well cooked. Add seasoning, **Chinese spice** or **curry powder** or **chilli** or anything to taste. Liquidise and serve with **parmesan** or **cream** or sprinkle with **chives** or **vegetable crisps**.

Beetroot Soup with Parmesan Mint Crisps

Ingredients

1 med – lge red onion

4 med raw beetroot

2 large cloves of garlic

1 vegetable stock cube

1½ pints hot beetroot water

Juice of half a lemon

1 tbsp olive oil

Knob of butter

Salt and pepper

Splash of double cream or crème fraiche (optional for a creamier taste)

Peel and cook raw beets in boiling water until soft, set aside. In a separate jug dissolve the stock cube in the beetroot water. Fry chopped onion and garlic in the oil and butter until soft and golden. Chop beetroot into small pieces and add to the pan. Add stock water to pan and simmer for 15 minutes.

Leave to cool, then liquidize, add the lemon juice, salt and pepper to taste.

Reheat and serve with Parmesan Crisps

Parmesan Crisps
Ingredients

Parmesan cheese

Fresh mint leaves

Black pepper

Finely grate parmesan cheese. Finely chop mint leaves and mix together with the parmesan, add black pepper. Pile mixture onto greaseproof paper into neat strips. Bake for 5 minutes in preheated oven 150°C/300°F/Gas 2, until cheese is melted.

Take out of the oven and carefully loosen the strips from the greaseproof paper, leave to cool.

Recipe and food styling
Michelle Wardingley

Two Rush Bearings

Hundreds of years ago, church floors were just bare earth, strewn with *rushes*.

By the end of summer, the rushes were in a bad way and, as grass and rushes are plentiful at this time, fresh ones were cut and spread to keep things warm, clean and sweet-smelling.

Every village had its *rush cart* and thousands of reeds would be piled on as it made its way through the streets, drawn by local men who would deliver the *new floors to the churches* and quench their thirst at the *ale houses* on the way.

In *Saddleworth* and thereabouts, the tradition had faded by the end of the 19th century but was briefly revived in 1906 for the *Saddleworth Wakes*, the annual holiday for the local mill and factory workers.

It lapsed again until 1978, when it re-started on the *first Saturday and Sunday in September*.

The cart is piled to 15 feet or more with rushes and pulled by up to *100 Morris men*. The streets are steep, so another 50 men are needed to restrain the cart on downhill stretches!

On top of the cart sits the *'jockey'* – a Morris man who shouts encouragement to the others and doesn't have to pull the cart. He tends to be last in the pub, mind.

Rush bearing at *Sowerby Bridge* is a bit different, in that the jockey is a girl – an especially brave one, considering the height of the rush pile and the steep cobbled streets.

The procession starts on Saturday morning from the *canal basin*. Sixty harnessed men sporting white shirts, black trousers, panama hats and wooden clogs pull the *16 foot tall decorated rush cart* along a spectacular 10 mile route, calling at churches and pubs on the way, encouraged by music, revellers, hundreds of followers in *Edwardian dress* and not a little ale.

The procession is entertained at stopping points by teams of Morris men from all around the country, dancing in a variety of regional styles.

In Sowerby Bridge itself, there is a riot of entertainment – a charity and craft market, local artists and dance groups and the *Friendly Band* (Friendly is a place as well as an appropriate adjective).

On Sunday, a festival service is held at *St. Peter's Church* and the procession then moves along the road to *Ripponden,* where it is welcomed to the village fair and *flower festival,* which is already in full swing. The *Pork Pie Appreciation Society* are on hand with pies and mushy peas.

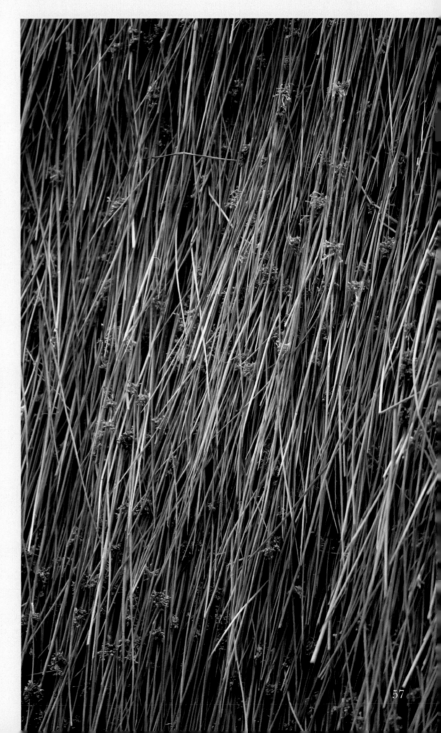

Lilly Berry Tart

We named this rustic tart Lilly Berry after noticing this name on the bench by the door at Deanhead Church. Joan Wheelwright (nee Berry) dedicated the bench in memory of her mother

Ingredients

1 and a half breakfast cupfuls of mixed **seasonal berries, Bilberries, Blackberries, Redcurrants, Cranberries** (200g approx) – if using frozen or tinned make sure they are well drained.

1(350g) pack chilled shortcrust pastry

4 tbsps caster sugar

4 egg yolks beaten

4 tbs double cream

Egg yolk and sprinkle of brown sugar for pastry glaze

Fresh bay leaves (optional)

8" foil baking tray

Heat oven to 180°C/350°F/ Gas Mark 4

Mix together fruit and sugar in a bowl.

Grease the foil baking tray, and line with the pastry, allowing some to hang over the edges, prick bottom of pastry base, place upturned spoons (large teaspoons or pudding spoons) inside the pie base and fold gently the additional pastry over, to create a rustic look. This will stop the pastry collapsing whilst cooking. Bake blind for 15–20 minutes.

Set aside to cool slightly and then remove spoons and the baking beans carefully. Fill the pastry case with the fruit lifting the rough edges of pastry gently, and fill to the edges. Brush pastry with a little egg yolk and sprinkle with brown sugar.

Beat together the egg yolks and cream, then pour over the fruit.

Cook for 25–30 minutes in moderate oven or until the egg mixture is cooked but slightly wobbly. Have a peek after 10 mins or so and if the pastry shows signs of browning cover with a collar of baking foil.

Decorate with leaves.
Serve cool, with a dollop of cream

Alice's Vegetable Pudding

by Alice R Thomas – Janet's sister

Ingredients

5 trimmed leeks, sliced

1 med red onion, chopped fine

6oz chestnut mushrooms

¼ tsp garlic paste

Salt and black pepper

Butter or butter oil

1½lbs sliced potatoes par boiled in salted water

4 large eggs

¾ pint milk

6 thick slices of bread of your choice

Sauté the red onions, garlic paste, salt and pepper in the butter until the onions have caramelised. Add the leeks and continue to fry, and then add the mushrooms chopped up small. In an ovenproof dish put a layer of the sliced potatoes, then add the leek mixture, and layer the remaining sliced potatoes on top. Pour over the 2 eggs that have been whisked ¼ pint of the milk.

Butter the bread on both sides and cut 2 slices in half diagonally and 2 slices into to quarters making smaller triangles. The large triangles of bread should be placed down the middle of the dish and the small triangles should fit down each side until all the mixture is covered. Pour on the 2 eggs that have been whisked with the remainder of the milk (1/2 pint) over the bread making sure that all the bread is soaked.

Place in oven reg 6 /200°C for 30 to 40 minutes.

Buck Rarebit

Traditionally a rarebit, or rabbit, is a tasty version of cheese on toast with either ale or wine added

Ingredients

50g/2oz butter

1 tsp wholegrain mustard

Pinch of sweet paprika

Salt and freshly ground pepper

175g/6oz mature cheddar cheese, grated

2 eggs

1 tbsp light ale

2 large rounds of bread

2-3 tsp Worcester sauce

Few drops of vinegar

Butter or margarine for greasing

Freshly ground black pepper

Heat the grill to high.
Cream together the butter, mustard, paprika and salt and pepper to taste.

Stir in the grated cheese and ale and add the Worcester sauce to taste. Stir again.

Fill a shallow saucepan three quarters full with boiling water add a few drops of vinegar and a pinch of salt, put the lid on the pan until the water returns to a rolling boil. Crack the eggs into the water and place the lid back on the pan. Take off the heat after 30 seconds. Leave the eggs in the water with the lid on for 3 to 7 minutes.

Meanwhile toast the bread, then spread on the cheese topping, take care not to spread right to the edges. Place under the hot grill for 3-4 minutes or until the topping has melted and is golden brown.

Place the prepared rarebits on warmed plates and top each with a poached egg. Season to taste. Serve immediately.

Serves 2

English Rarebit – 1795

Toast a slice of **brown bread** on both sides and lay it on a plate before the fire. Pour over it a **glass of red wine** and leave to soak in. Cut some **cheese** very thin and lay it thickly over the bread. Place in a tin oven before the fire and it will, presently be toasted and brown.

A Valuable Turnip

Harvest Festival at St. Bartholomew's

The *Harvest Festival at Dean Head Church* on the hillside above *Scammonden Water* is a real community occasion. The church is always packed with home, farm, garden and hand made produce, plus the locals who have brought it all to decorate the church.

The action moves to the *Cricket Club* (or sometimes a local pub) in the evening, where *David Jackson* and the *Haigh brothers* from the *Honley Male Voice Choir* entertain with soulful songs, including *'Oh to be a farmers boy'*, and everyone enjoys *Mrs Parker's* famous meat pie and mushy peas.

Then follows the auction, at which produce from church is sold off in aid of charity.

Among the crafts, chrysanths cakes and marrows there's sometimes a salt wheatsheaf bread, which prompts great bidding rivalry, but the most valuable item in the sale each year is the *turnip*.

Why? Well, because it's passed around along with a *hammer*, everyone *bangs a coin into the flesh*.

As it gets heavier, it becomes more valuable, and when everyone has had a turn with the hammer, the turnip is sold to the highest bidder.

It's always the last and the most expensive single item, though the cannier members of the crowd never over-bid. You can spot them watching its progress around the room, trying to calculate the currency content so as to *make a profit on their bid!*

The winner of the turnip then rushes home to put on the oven on, as the approved way to *release its value* is to bake it!

Harvest Festival
Salt Bread Wheat Sheaf

For decoration only – if you do wish to make it edible then only use a pinch of salt

Ingredients
900g/2lb unbleached white
Bread flour
15ml/1 tbsp salt
15g/½oz fresh yeast
75ml/5 tbsps lukewarm milk
400ml/14 fl oz cold water

For the glaze
15ml/1 tbsp milk
1 egg

In a large bowl sift the flour and salt together and make a well in the centre. Cream the yeast with the milk and add to the centre of the flour with the water and mix to a stiff dough. Knead on a lightly floured surface until smooth and elastic, about 10-15 minutes. Leave to rest in a lightly oiled bowl and covered with cling film at room temperature for about 2 hours, or until the dough has doubled in size.

Knock back and knead on a lightly floured surface for 1 minute, then cover and leave to rest for 10 minutes

Split the dough in two. Roll one half to a 35x24cm/14x10inch oblong, and then loosely fold in half lengthways. With a sharp knife cut out a half mushroom shape for the sheaf, leaving the folded edge uncut. The stalk base should be 18cm/7inches long. Reserve the off cuts for the braided rope.

Place the dough on a lightly greased baking sheet (at least 38x33cm/15x13 inches) Prick with a fork and brush with water, cover and put to one side.

Beat the egg and milk together for the glaze. On a lightly floured surface, roll out the remaining dough to 28x18cm/11x7inches and cut into approx 35 thin strips of 18cm/7 inches in length. Place these as close as possible side-by-side length ways on the prepared base as these will be the wheat stalks. Brush with some of the glaze.

Roll the 'off cut' dough to make six strips of 43cm/17" long. Make in to two plaits and then place one at each side of the wheat stalks tying them together in the middle.

Take the remaining larger piece of dough and cut a 7cm/3inch strip from one end and reserve covered up. Split what is left into four, and then further divide each of these quarters into about 25 oblong rolls, to eventually represent 100 wheat ears. Make one end of these rolls pointed. Snip with scissors each side of each roll with a diagonal cut to create the wheatear shapes.

Arrange the ears around the top outer edge of the mushroom shaped base. Repeat a second row lower down by placing dough ears between the upper ears. Repeat until all the ears have been used.

Brush with the glaze as you go to stop the dough from drying out. Using a sharp knife prick in between the ears and stalks and bake for 15 minutes at 220°C/425°F/Gas 7. Brush with the remaining glaze Reduce the oven to 120°C/250°F/Gas ½ for several hours until the dough dries out. Remove and allow to cool on the baking sheet.

Scammonden's Sizzling Sausage Sunday

Around mid summers day *Deanhead church* hosts another fund raising family day, with *Mr Duncan Newsome* offering his home made sausages, usually five different varieties! And the *Friendly Brass Band* accompaniment the games and jubilations

The Friendly Band is a brass band based in *Friendly Sowerby Bridge*, near *Halifax*. The band has a long history dating back to *1868*, and continues to take a play a very active role in the brass band world, taking part in many contests, a wide range of other public engagements and a variety of private functions such as weddings and birthday parties.

.... and not forgetting to mention *The SAS – The Sausage Appreciation Society*. This meets at the *Lower Royal George* every Thursday evening.

If you're lucky you will be invited to try any surplus sausages – but be warned there is a long waiting list of gentlemen wishing to join the SAS!

Britain's Star Sausage Competition starts at the beginning of August and closes after a month. The results are celebrated at *The British Sausage Week* which begins on the *1st November*. The road show travels the country to crown the regional finalists.

Sausage and Spring Mash Pie

A Family recipe from Ruth Dean, Far Barsey Farm Shop.

Ingredients

1½kg potatoes cut in chunks

100ml/3½floz milk

¼ to ½ shredded savoy cabbage

50g/2oz butter

1 tbsp wholegrain mustard

2 tsp vegetable oil

16 Far Barsdey Classic Pork Sausage

2-3 sprigs of Thyme

10 shallots peeled and halved

4 carrots thickly sliced

500g mushrooms

400ml/14 fl oz red wine

99ml/½pt beef stock

2 tbsps caramelised onions

Boil the potatoes in salted water (approx 15 mins). Add cabbage for the last 5 mins of cooking, drain, add butter, mustard and mash all together.

While the potatoes are boiling, heat the oil in a shallow flameproof dish or frying pan. Brown the sausages, shallots and carrots until golden and shallots start to soften. Ensure the sausages are cooked through. Lift out the sausages in to the serving dish.

Tip off any excess fat from the pan and add the mushrooms and thyme, cook for 3 mins, add red wine, then allow to reduce by half. Add stock and caramelised onions. Reduce a little more until shiny, and then pour over the sausages. Top with mash potato mixture.

Bake in oven covered 30 mins (200 °C/fan 180 Gas). Remove the cover and allow to brown in the final 10 mins. Serves 6 – 8.

All ingredients available at Far Barsey Farm Shop

Marsden Cuckoo Festival

Marsden is a small town tucked away under Saddleworth Moor in the Colne Vallley

It is important for the people living in the *Pennines* to look for the signs that the long harsh winters are turning in to spring.

Many years ago the people of *Marsden* were aware that along with the *snowdrops and daffodils* the sunshine came and the sound of the first cuckoo marked traditionally the signal that spring had finally arrived. This is heard in the valley around the time of *Marsden Spring Cattle Fair.*

Essence of Hawthorn

This makes delicious flavouring for creams and custards, or it may be used as a liqueur.

Hawthorn or May blossom Brandy

Take some petals of hawthorn when they at there best and freshest, and put them in a scrupulously clean and dry bottle, filling it about three quarters full. Fill up with good Brandy, and cork tightly.

Keep this in a cool place for three or four weeks, and then strain off in to another bottle.

In order to try and prolong the stay of the cuckoo they built a wall around it. Sadly the wall wasn't high enough and the cuckoo flew away *…it were nobbut just wun course too low!*

The event which was formally called *Cuckoo Day* starts on the *Friday (around 27th April)* with a guided walk setting off from the *Mechanics Hall* for a hard 2 mile walk to the birthplace of the cuckoo legend. A folk evening usually follows. On the Saturday afternoon there is the *Grand Cuckoo Procession,* consisting of large cuckoos nesting on straw beds in trailers pulled by farm vehicles. Children from local schools have also revived the tradition of *wheelbarrow floats* also.

During the day amongst the many highlights of the festival are dance and theatre groups, fairground rides, stalls, a craft fair, a duck race and most importantly the traditional procession of the *Marsden Silver prize Band.*

Eveline Ainleys Cake

Ingredients

4oz margarine

3oz fine brown sugar

**1 tbsp maple syrup
(or golden syrup)**

1 egg

6oz self raising flour

2 tbsps milk

2oz chopped walnuts

Cream together margarine and sugar. Sieve the sugar to avoid lumps. Add the beaten egg, and then the Syrup, Mix together to form a smooth mixture. Add milk, and fold in the sieved flour.

Break up the walnuts to smaller pieces, add to the mixture. Line a baking tin with grease proof paper, smooth in the cake mixture and bake in the oven for 25–30 minutes on 280 preheated oven, until golden brown and the cake is soft and spongy to touch.

Ainley Topping

Ingredients

4oz icing sugar

1 tsp coffee granules

2oz soft butter

2 tbs hot water

**Handful of chopped walnuts
to decorate**

Mix together butter and icing sugar until smooth. Add coffee mixture to taste. Smooth over top of cake and decorate with chopped walnuts.

Eveline Ainley is Michelle Wardingley's maternal Grandmother.

The Norland Scarecrow Trail

This is a four-day event that's held at the same time as the *Sowerby Rush Bearing* – usually the first weekend in *September*.

It began as a *Millennium celebration in 2000* and has continued ever since, bringing what is quite a widespread community together and raising money for charity and local good causes.

The first theme was nursery rhymes and few locals will forget *Humpty Dumpty*, the cow that jumped over the moon and *Little Miss Muffet* complete with a terrifying spider hanging from a tree above her head!

The competition has gathered pace in the last decade and these days you can count on seeing over *80 scarecrows* along the trail.

Themes such as films, jobs and Disney characters have brought out the creativity and competitive spirit of *Norland folk* and the scarecrow standard gets higher every year.

There is tragedy too, mind. In 2009, cows ate one of the scarecrows – an event so traumatic that it made local headlines.

If you go, don't miss the sideshows, fun fair and cream teas and also the sandwiches at the church.

Apple & Vanilla Sponge

A family recipe from Ruth Dean. Far Barsey Farm shop

Ingredients

250g/9oz unsalted butter or marg

250g/9oz golden caster sugar

4 eggs beaten

250g/9oz self raising flour

1 splash vanilla essence

2 tbsps demerara sugar

**2 medium Bramley apples
(peeled and cut in to wedges)**

¼ tsp ground cinnamon

Heat the oven to 180°fan/Gas 4. Line a 8"cake tin with baking paper (loose bottom tin).

Beat together butter and caster sugar till the mixture turns pale and fluffy. Add the eggs, flour and vanilla. Beat together until smooth.

Tip in to prepared tin, lay apple wedges on top and poke them half way down into the cake mixture (the apples look crowded, but shrink as they cook). Sprinkle with demerara sugar and cinnamon. Bake for approx 1 hour 5mins until risen and golden and the skewer comes out clean.

Leave for a few mins before taking from the tin and cooling on a wire tray.

This moist cake can also be eaten as a delicious pudding served with custard, cream or ice cream.

Lemon Tart

Ingredients

For the pastry

175g plain flour

Large pinch of salt

75g icing sugar

90g very cold cubed butter

1 egg yolk

2 tbs cold water

For the Filling

4 eggs

175g golden caster sugar

finely grated zest of 2 lemons

100ml double cream

Juice of 2 lemons (approx 100ml)

Pre heat baking sheet in oven
190°C/375°F/Gas 5

Mix the egg yolk and cold water. Rub the flour, salt, sugar and butter together. Add the egg yolk and stir with a fork. When the pastry begins to bind together turn out on to a floured surface and knead for a few seconds. Roll out the pastry to ½ cm thick and fit in to a 24cm loose bottomed fluted flan tin. Trim off the excess pastry leaving a 1 cm border. Chill in the freezer for 10 mins, Cook blind for 10 mins.

Remove greaseproof paper and baking beans, trim edges again and bake for a further 8-10 mins. Reduce the oven temperature to 160°C/325°F/Gas 3.

Whisk the eggs and sugar together. Stir in the double cream, lemon juice and zest. Pour the filling mixture in to the pastry case and bake for 35 to 40 mins.

Be on hand with some baking foil to cover the pastry if necessary. When the filling is almost set, but still wobbles very slightly the tart is ready. As the tart cools the filling will set. Leave to cool completely, then remove from the tin.

Dust with icing sugar

Marsden Imbolc

Imbolc pronounced *im-olk* celebrates the first signs of spring with purification and fire. Imbolc is an Irish word meaning *'in the belly'* which *Irish festivals* celebrate at the beginning of February. It can also be known as *St Brigid's Day* as it is dedicated to the goddess *Brighid*.

In *Marsden,* it's a spectacular affair. The week before, residents and visitors attend fire swinging and lantern making workshops and on the night of the festival itself, the sky lights up as a torchlight procession winds its way from the railway station to the end of the *Standedge Canal Tunnel*.

This is the highest, longest and deepest canal tunnel in the UK, stretching for over 3 miles through hard millstone grit to take the *Huddersfield Narrow Canal* from *Marsden* through to *Diggle* in Lancashire.

Follow the procession and you'll see elaborate fire sculptures and even a fire circus, with fire juggling and, of course, fire-eaters.

The finale is quite terrifying – the annual fight to the death between *Jack Frost* and the *Green Man*.

Cinder Toffee

Shirley Sidall

Ingredients
25g butter, unsalted
200g caster sugar
4 tbsp golden syrup
1 tbs bicarb soda

Grease a 20cm square tin with butter.

Melt the sugar and golden syrup together in a heavy based saucepan over a low heat. Bring the heat up to medium and simmer for 3 to 4 minutes.

When the mixture is thick and a dark caramel colour remove from the heat – immediately whisk in the bicarbonate of soda so that the mixture froths up (great fun!). Pour into a tin and leave to set at room temperature for approx 2 – 3 hours.

When the toffee has set, bash the now honeycomb into large pieces

Hot Toddy

Ingredients

Large measure of Whisky

Two tsps of brown sugar

Mixed dried fruit

Method

Mix together the Whisky, fruit and sugar in a cup. Pour over boiled water, stir together.

Add a slice of lemon and stir with a cinnamon stick

Lamb and Rosemary Stew with Spinach

I came up with this recipe when I had a glut of home grown ingredients; using plenty of rosemary gives a wonderful aromatic flavour

Ingredients

1½lbs /800g stewing lamb

Handful of fresh rosemary leaves, finely chopped

Sea salt and freshly ground black pepper

2 heaped tbsps of flour

2 tbsps of extra virgin olive oil

1 onion, peeled and roughly chopped

8oz/200g button mushrooms roughly sliced

1 large carrot roughly chopped

1lb/450 g new potatoes par boiled and cut into bite size pieces

1 pint /570ml hot stock

½ pint/275 ml light ale

5oz/125g (approx) spinach washed, torn with stalks removed

Pre heat oven to 180°C/350°F/Gas 4

Place the lamb in a bowl and season well with the salt and pepper, add the flour and chopped rosemary and mix until all the meat is completely coated.

Heat the oil in a casserole type pan and in batches gently brown the lamb pieces. Remove from the pan and set aside. Turn the heat down and then fry the onions, mushrooms and carrot for about 5 minutes until all have softened and are slightly coloured.

Return the lamb to the pan along with the stock and ale. Bring to the boil and simmer for about 20 minutes. Put the covered pan in the oven for about 1 ½ hours or until the lamb falls apart.

Stir in the spinach leaves until they begin to wilt.

Serve with crusty bread

Bacon, Egg & Potato Pie

This pie can be a breakfast meal or may be served hot or cold at any time of the day

Ingredients

6 large free-range eggs

1lb/500g salad potatoes

1lb/500g/ of rindless bacon

1½lbs /700g shortcrust pastry

1 egg or milk for the pastry glaze

Pre heat the oven to 200°C.

Lightly grease an 8 inch ovenproof dish. Boil the potatoes until soft and when slightly cooled slice.

Lightly fry the bacon. Prepare the pastry glaze by beating the egg or having a little milk ready.

Roll out the pastry into two squares, one roughly 12 inches and the other 8½ inches. Line the prepared oven dish with the large square of pastry, making sure that the pastry is snugly and gently pressed in the bottom and sides of the dish. The pastry should also hang over the edge.

Place the sliced potatoes in 2 or 3 layers, then layer up the bacon slices. Crack each of the eggs evenly spaced on top of the bacon.

Brush the pastry rim of the pie with the egg/milk and carefully place the pastry lid on top very gently pressing down with your fingers. Brush the top of the pie with more egg/milk wash and press round the rim of the pastry with a fork or back of a teaspoon.

Using a sharp knife cut several small incisions in middle of the pastry lid to enable the steam to escape. Be careful not to puncture the egg yolks!

Bake at 200°C /400°F/Gas 6 for 15 minutes, then reduce the heat and bake until golden brown, approx 45 minutes.

Serves 6

A Marsden story

as told by Mike Grange's grandmother

Around 1910, there was a lady butcher in *Marsden* named *Bathsheba*. People called her Bashiba, with emphasis on the two a's.

A customer once complained about the high proportion of bone (as opposed to flesh) in the meat she was buying and Bashiba retorted – *"It's bo an as gets 'em to t'market."*

In those days, cattle and sheep walked to market, driven along droveways for sometimes many miles. Even geese had to get market under their own steam and some geese walked all the way from *Norfolk to the London* markets.

Mike continues;
"As a freeman of the *Worshipful Company of Clockmakers* I am permitted to drive my sheep across London Bridge – I have never tried it yet!"

Mike Grange who has become a very dear friend of ours had a collection of nearly 150 30 hour long case clocks that he has now donated to the *British Museum*. His fascination and love for these clocks began as a small boy when his father came home one day with a *John Stancliffe* 30 hour clock. John Stancliffe the clockmaker lived and made his clocks in *Lower Woodhead, Barkisland* in the 1750's.

Yorkshire Sauce

A sauce to be used with cold roast meats. Use salted dry anchovies if you can get them or drain off oil from tinned ones, wash and pat dry.

Ingredients

2 x 50g /2 oz tins of anchovies

4 garlic cloves peeled and chopped

4 shallots, peeled and chopped

1 tbsp brown sugar

1 tsp ground mace

½ tsp ground all spice

3 tbsps dark soy sauce

1 tsp cayenne pepper

1 litre/2 pints malt vinegar

2 tbsps mushroom ketchup (optional)

Whizz all ingredients together in a food processor, except the malt vinegar, for a few seconds.

Put in to large jars, add the vinegar and cover. Shake every day for a month. Strain through muslin and bottle.

Food styling Jo Brewer

Yorkshire Pudding

Serves 3 to 4 people

A batter pudding that became popular in the early part of the 18th century – batter puddings being mostly sweet at that time – *The Yorkshire Pudding* was also called *'A Dripping Pudding'* in *The Whole Duty of a Woman' 1737*, when meat was roasted on a spit, or by suspending it from a jack in front of the fire.

A dish was placed a few inches below the joint to catch the juices and when smoking hot the batter would be poured in to the roasting dish and as a consequence forming a crust straight away. When the pudding begins to cook the all-important air that's in the batter during mixing expands, making it rise and the fierce heat dries out the top of the pudding making it crunchy.

Yorkshire people frequently say that southerners are unable to make a proper *Yorkshire Pudding,* possibly as it has been reputed that 19th century cookery writers distorted and misunderstood and never tasted the true Yorkshire Pudding!

The true Yorkshire Pudding should be cut into squares and served with gravy before the meat to take the edge off the appetite! It is however now the traditional accompaniment for roast beef in *Britain,* but it was eaten with any meat and the appropriate sauce (mint for lamb, apple for pork)

Ingredients

4oz plain flour

2 eggs

½ pint milk

Pinch of salt

2 or 3 tbsps of beef dripping (or 1 oz lard or of bacon fat)

Sieve the flour and salt into a basin, and make a well in the centre. Drop in the two yolks of eggs, and with a wooden spoon mix a little of the flour into them. Then add about half the milk very gradually, mixing in the flour by degrees from the sides of the basin. Keep the batter thick enough to allow all lumps rubbed smooth and beat in well until it is full of air bubbles. Add the rest of the milk, and stand for half an hour at least.

Just at the last, stir in quickly and lightly the whites of the eggs beaten to a stiff froth. Place the beef dripping (hot dripping from the roast is best) in a Yorkshire pudding tin, (or a tin size 9½ x 7½ inches) make it quite hot (take care it should be boiling or hazing) in the oven and run it over the tin. Then pour in the batter and cook in a quick oven (200°C or Gas mark 6) for about 35 to 40 mins until brown and crisp.

Food styling Sandra Beasley

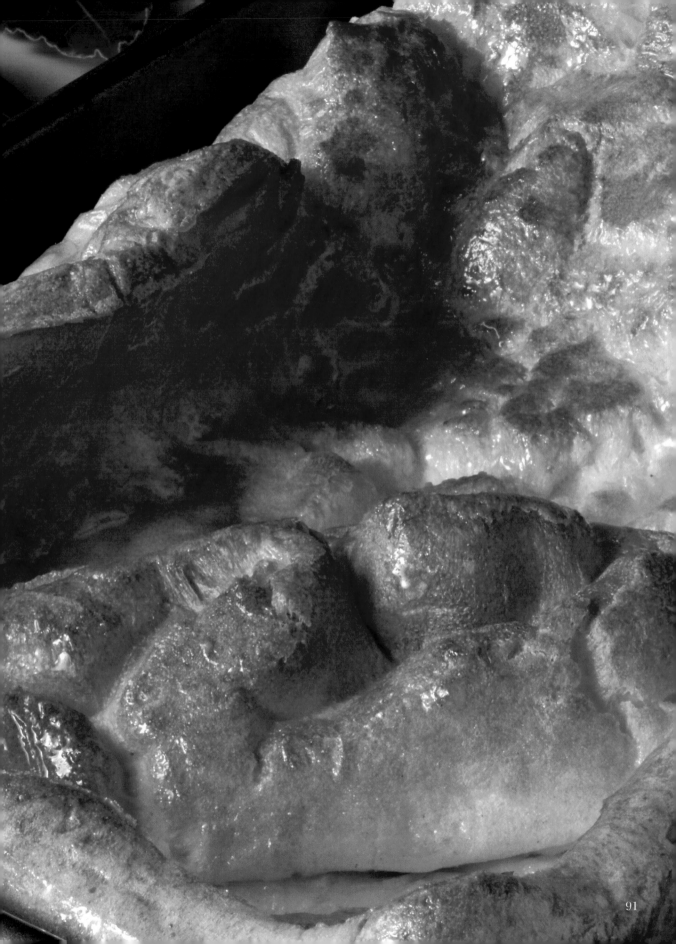

Lamb Shank

Susie Creane-Smith, Tannochbrae Restaurant

Ingredients
4 lamb shanks (all the same size)
1 medium onion chopped
4 large cloves of garlic chopped

Heat the oven to 160°C Gas 3

Fry the lamb shanks and brown all over. Remove and place in ovenproof casserole. Fry the onions and garlic in the same pan and add to the casserole.

Serves 4

For the sauce

Ingredients
2 bay leaves
A few sprigs of rosemary
1 handful mint leaves
20 juniper berries
3 tbsps redcurrant jelly
1 bottle of red wine
1 pint of lamb stock
1 tbsp Worcester sauce
Zest and juice of 1 orange
Juice of ½ lemon

Add all the sauce ingredients to the casserole and cover and cook in oven for 2 hours until the lamb is very tender.

Remove the lamb from the casserole and keep warm. Remove the herbs and blend the sauce until smooth return to the pan and reduce until it begins to thicken.

Serve the sauce poured over the lamb with creamy mashed potatoes and mint sauce.

Food styling Susie Creane-Smith

Mother Eve's Pudding

Eve's Pudding is a modern name for a sponge pudding with lemon and vanilla flavouring which has chopped apples underneath. It is a descendant of the *Duke of Cumberland's* pudding from the 18th century, which is a boiled pudding with the apples inside and not underneath.

The pudding that surrounded the apples was made of a suet mixture with a lot of eggs. The pudding was served with melted butter, wine and sugar.

19th - anon

"If you would have a good pudding, observe what you're taught. Take *two pennyworth of eggs,* when twelve for the groat, and of the same fruit that Eve had once chosen, well pared and well chopped, at least half a dozen; Six ounces of bread (let your maid eat the crust), the crumbs must be grated as *small as the dust;*

Six ounces of currants from the stones you must sort, lest they *break out your teeth*, and spoil all your sport; Five ounces of sugar won't make it too sweet; Some salt and some nutmeg will make it complete; Three hours to boil, without hurry or flutter, then serve it up without sugar or butter."

Eve's Pudding

Ingredients

4oz flour

1lb cooking apples

2oz butter

5oz sugar

1 lemon

1 egg

A little butter (optional)

½ tsp baking powder

A little milk

Peel core and slice the apples, put them in a saucepan with a little water, a little butter (this improves the flavour) and 2oz of the sugar and the grated rind and juice of ½ a lemon. Simmer until softened. Put the apples in the bottom of a pie dish – packing the apples down provides a firm base for the topping and helps it rise evenly during baking

Sieve the flour, pinch of salt and baking powder. In a separate bowl cream the butter and the remaining sugar, beat in the egg and then fold in the flour lightly, adding a little milk if required.

Pour the mixture on top of the apple and bake in a moderate oven for 45 minutes to an hour.

Serve with custard or cream

Lemon Posset

by Susie Creane-Smith, Tannochbrae Restaurant

Ingredients

600ml/1 pint double cream

Zest and juice of two lemons

150g/5oz caster sugar (or golden caster sugar for a deeper colour)

Place in a large pan the double cream and the sugar and bring to the boil slowly over a low heat. Boil for three minutes, then remove from the heat and allow to cool. Add the lemon juice and zest and whisk well. Pour the lemon cream into 6 large serving glasses or 12 shot glasses and refrigerate for 3 hours. Dust with icing sugar and serve with raspberry coulis or fresh berries.

In Medieval England, a posset was a sweetened, lightly curdled milk drink. The slight curdling would occur with the addition of an acid liquid, this might have been wine, ale or citrus juice. It was then sweetened and sometimes spiced.

This is the modern version, which is just like a rich lemon curd. May be served with tiny-spiced shortbread fingers for a real treat!

Slaithwaite Moonraking Festival

Over 200 years ago, a band of smugglers were bringing barrels of illicit alcohol by boat along the *Huddersfield Narrow Canal* when they saw an approaching *constable*.

To avoid arrest they pushed the cargo over the side of the boat.

Later that evening, they returned under a full moon to retrieve the barrels by raking them to the bank. That same *constable* was on patrol and challenged them again.

They avoided arrest by pretending to be drunk, saying that the *moon had fallen into the canal* and they were trying to rake it out.

To prove their claim, they pointed to the moon's reflection, clearly visible in the water.

Nowadays, the citizens of *Slaithwaite* celebrate this escape from justice with a week of processions and re-enactments every other February.

Now here are a couple of intriguing facts about *Slaithwaite,* courtesy of my friend *Jo Brewer* who lives there and is very careful with her pronunciation.

First, how to say it: to sound like a local, you must say *'Slawit'* or *'Slathwaite'*. Early spelling was *'Slathuait'*.

If you say *'Slay-thwayte'* they'll know you're a foreigner or even from Surrey.

There is a *Lewisham Road* in Slaithwaite, and a Slaithwaite Road in *Lewisham*. This exchange of names commemorates the marriage between a local and a London family. Lewisham Road Slaithwaite was once known as Brasshandle Street, because of its elegance.

Slaithwaite's big house is Linthwaite Hall, built by the *Lockwood family* around 1600 on the site of the manor house of the *de Lynthwaites*. The hall is haunted and is said to have a secret passage that leads out of the house and straight into *Kitchen Fold* in *Slaithwaite*.

Cocktails

A cocktail nearly always needs ice.
But never use the same ice twice!
Shake the shaker vigorously to make the cocktail come alive.
Use a shaker with plenty of space to shake in!
If you can, chill your glasses first.
Drink your cocktail as soon as possible.

Moonraker Cocktail

Pour in to the shaker **2 glasses of Brandy, 2 of Quinquina** (generic name for sweetened fortified aperitif wines containing quinine and spices – major brands Dubonnet and St.Raphael. The quinine is the bitter constituent which promotes the production of enzymes and, therefore appetite) and **2 of Peach Brandy**. Add **3 dashes of Absinthe**, shake vigorously and serve.
(six people)

Raspberry Wine

from Mary Moon, Jo's neighbour in Linthwaite

Ingredients

1kg ripe raspberries

250g red grape juice

1kg sugar

4 litres water

1 campden tablet

¼ tsp pectic enzyme

Wash the raspberries. Pour the cold water over them. Add campden tablet and pectic enzyme. Cover. Leave for the next day. Stir in grape juice and sugar. Leave in a warm place for 6-7 days. Strain in to a Demi-John. Then leave for a week. Strain. Repeat until the wine clears.

Blackberry Wine

Ingredients

4lb blackberries

1 gallon boiling water

Yeast nutrient – 1 tsp to the gallon (available from home brew suppliers)

3lb granulated sugar

Yeast (1 tsp) or phial general-purpose yeast)

The fruit should be picked when ripe on a dry sunny day. Wash it well, being careful to remove any of the small maggots sometimes found in blackberries. Place the fruit in a crock and crush with a wooden spoon. Pour over a gallon of boiling water. Stir well and allow to become luke warm. (about 70 deg. F.) Then add the yeast. Cover closely and leave for 1 to 5 days, stirring daily.

Strain through 2 thicknesses of muslin (or nylon sieve) on to 3lbs granulated sugar, and add the yeast nutrient. Stir well to make sure all is dissolved. Pour in to a dark fermenting jar or "grey hen", filling to the shoulder and fit fermentation trap or plug of cotton wool. When the fermentation quietens sufficiently for there to be no risk of it foaming through the trap (say after 1 week) top up with the spare wine to base of the neck and refit the trap. Leave until it clears and then rack for the first time.

Archbishop

Stick an **orange full of cloves** and roast it before the fire or in the oven. When brown, cut it in to quarters, remove the pips, and put in to a stew pan. Pour over a **bottle of claret**, and let it simmer for fifteen minutes.

Strain and serve.

Bishop

Bishop is made in the same way as Archbishop, but **Port** is used instead of claret.

Old English Punch

Rub a **rind of a lemon** on a **quarter of a pound of loafsugar**. Dissolve the sugar in boiling water, then add **half a pint of boiling ale**, a **gill of strong hot tea**, the **juice of a lemon**, and a **wine glass each of brandy and rum.**

Mix well

Cocktail Treats

These cocktail treats are so moreish – make sure you make enough!

Cocktail Cashews

Take some **Raw Shelled Cashews** and either stir-fry them in good flavoursome **oil** or simply roast them in the oven.

Once the cashews are lightly browned, serve hot, having tossed in one of the following;

**Salt and pepper or
smoked flavoured salt.
If frying add a little garlic or chilli
oil and then salt.**

Baby Yorkshire Puddings with Cocktail Sausages

Prepare **Yorkshire pudding mixture** as on page 92

Place **24 cocktail sausages** in a baking tin and cook until browned.

Meanwhile put ½ **teaspoonful of olive oil** in each of the 24 cases (non-stick or silicon mini muffin tins) place in the oven for 10 mins so the oil is hazing hot. Then quickly fill each case ⅔ full of the batter. Bake for 10 mins until puffed up and golden. Cool. When ready to use place in oven in a baking tray and place a cocktail sausage on each and bake for 5 mins until hot and puffed up. Serve hot with Horseradish sauce or Onion Relish page 30.

Piquant Pecans

Ingredients

½ cup melted butter

2 tsp garlic salt

4 cups Pecan halves

½ tsp Tabasco

4 tsp Worcester sauce

When the butter has melted add the salt, Tabasco and Worcester sauce. Stir in the Pecans so that they are well coated. Spread the nuts on baking sheet lined with grease proof paper and bake for about 25 minutes until crisp and browned in oven at 350°F. stirring occasionally. Drain on kitchen paper. Serve warm.

Curried Walnuts

Ingredients

¼ lb shelled walnuts

¼ cup olive oil

1 tbsp Worcester sauce

1 tbsp curry powder

**1 tbsp mango chutney,
put through a fine sieve**

dash cayenne (optional)

Lightly sauté the walnuts, add Worcester sauce and season. Bake for 20 minutes at 325°F in a shallow baking tray. Serve warm or cold.

Vegetable Curry

Ingredients

1 tbsp vegetable oil

1 small cauliflower cut in to florets

5oz/125g French beans

2 garlic cloves

1 inch fresh ginger

3 bay leaves

4 beef tomatoes roughly chopped

2 tbsps of frozen peas

A large pinch of salt and black pepper

1 pint vegetable stock

½ tsp of each of chilli, cumin, coriander, turmeric powders

1 tbsp smooth mango chutney

Peel and finely chop the garlic and ginger.

Heat the veg oil in a pan over a high heat. Quickly stir fry the garlic, ginger and onion for 2 minutes then add the french beans, cauliflower and the powders and stir fry for about 7 minutes or until the cauliflower is lightly browned, adding a drop of water if it begins to stick. Add peas, the chopped tomatoes and the stock and salt and pepper. When the cauliflower begins to soften remove from the heat and stir in the mango chutney.

Serve with rice

Slaithwaite Meat Tea

On or about the afternoon of the second *Saturday in March*, you'll see a little crowd of *Barkisland menfolk* at a local pub, waiting for the bus that takes them to *Slaithwaite Working Men's Club* for *The Meat Tea*.

The Meat Tea has been celebrated at Slaithwaite for over 200 years and although times aren't so hard these days and meat is usually eaten more than once a week, it's still a much-anticipated annual treat for which the chaps put by a little *'brass'* each week.

It's a rare honour for outsiders to be invited and the Barkisland contingent know how privileged they are.

The men all sit around a *U-shaped wooden table* and tuck into generous portions of beef, ham, pickles and buttered bread, served by local ladies who, until recently, wore white cotton bonnets.

This is followed by copious amounts of home made fruitcake, parkin, bakewell tart, butterfly buns and Yorkshire curd tart, all washed down with strong Yorkshire tea.

Those who can move after all this go down to the bar where there's usually a 'turn' on, plus horse racing games and dominoes.

Things get a bit hazy later, as much is supped and not a lot remembered or recounted – in mixed company at least!

It's a *'reet good do'* by all accounts, though I can't help wondering why the Slaithwaite ladies don't get to eat!

Wen lads 'ave brass,
they're men.
Wen they're spent up,
they're lads agen.

Halifax High Tea Beef

Ingredients

4lb piece of salted brisket of beef

½lb bacon pieces

2 carrots

1 onion

Savoury herbs

Stock

A good pinch of ground allspice, cloves and mace seasoning

Place all ingredients in an ovenproof dish and pour over stock. Cover with lid tightly and bake in a warm oven 160°C/325F/ Gas 6 for approximately 4 hours or until tender. Remove from the oven and allow to cool in the liquid. When cool remove the meat and place on a dish and weight down heavily and leave to press overnight. Turn out and serve cold.

Yorkshire Plum Bread

Ingredients

1lb flour

2oz peel

5oz sugar

6oz butter

2oz yeast

½ pint milk

1lb mixed raisins, currants and sultanas

Rub butter in to flour, add all dry ingredients. Dissolve the yeast in a little warm water, in which a little sugar is added and a shake of pepper (this brings up the yeast if not fresh).

Make a well in the centre of the flour mix and pour in warmed milk and then the yeast. Mix well.

Make three cuts with a knife in to the dough and cover with warm cloth for 20 – 30 mins to rise.

Have ready two loaf tins, warmed and greased slightly. Divide the mixture between the tins and let them rise for a further 20 mins, then bake slowly in an oven for one hour. Cut in slices and butter.

Diggers

(similar to a Brandy Snap, but more nutritious)

Ingredients

2 breakfast cupful of oat flakes

1 breakfast cupful of sugar

1 breakfast cupful of flour

4 ozs butter

2 tbsps Golden Syrup

½ tsp ginger

1 tsp bicarbonate of soda

Pinch of salt

Warm the butter, sugar, and golden syrup and mix together. Add the dry ingredients. Scald the soda with a little boiling water, and mix in to a fairly stiff paste. Drop in to cake tins, and bake in a moderate oven until golden brown.

Yorkshire Cheesecake

This recipe is over 150 years old.

Ingredients

3oz each of – butter, sugar and currants

1 hard boiled egg finely chopped

1 dessertspoonful ground rice

1 egg

* A little flavouring

Line the plates or small tartlet tins with puff or short pastry. Place the mixture on the pastry. Cook in a moderate oven.

* In recent times a little lemon curd has been spread on the pastry hence curd tart.

Traditional Yorkshire Curd Tart

Ingredients

225g/8oz plain flour

Large pinch of ground allspice

1 egg yolk

115g/4oz soft brown sugar

115g/4oz butter diced

3 eggs beaten

Grated rind and juice of one lemon

50g/2oz butter, melted

450g/1lb medium soft fat cheese

115g/4oz sultanas

Preheat the oven to 190°C / 375°F/Gas 5.

Toss the butter in the flour, then rub it in until the mixture resembles breadcrumbs, stir the egg yolk into the flour mixture with a little water to bind it together. Turn the dough onto a lightly floured surface, knead lightly and briefly, then form into a ball. Roll out the pastry thinly and use to line a 20cm/8in loose bottom flan tin, chill for 15 minutes.

To make the filling; mix the ground allspice with the sugar, then stir in the eggs, lemon rind and juice, butter, soft cheese and sultanas, pour the filling into the pastry case, then bake for about 40 minutes until the pastry is cooked and the filling is lightly set and golden brown. Serve slightly warm with cream.

Bakewell Tart

C 1900

Ingredients

4oz shortcrust pastry

Raspberry jam

2oz butter

2oz ground almonds

2oz sugar

1 egg

Line a pie plate with the pastry, spread with jam. Cream together butter and sugar, beat in the egg, add ground almonds. Spread the mixture on top of the pastry.

Bake at 180°C/Gas 4 for about 30-35 minutes.

Delicious also served warm with custard or cream.

Twelfth Night Cake

As the title suggests made for twelfth night celebrations or *Epiphany* when the three kings visited the infant *Jesus*. This festival, has inherited some *pagan customs* thrown back from the Romans, where the slaves were allowed many privileges such as eating and gambling with their masters.

A *dice* would be thrown to choose the king and for that evening everyone would have to obey his command. In other countries a *dried bean* or a *china doll* or a coin would be baked in the cake, and depending on the customs of the country the finder of this token was either privileged or had to pay *forfeits!*

From the *Oxford Companion of food: Bridget Ann Henisch* (1984) cities *Henry Teonge*, a naval Chaplin, who wrote in 1676 that : we had a great cake, made in which was put a bean for the King, *a pea for the Queen*, a clove for the knave, a forked stick for the cuckold, and a rag for the slut. The cake was then cut into several pieces in the great cabin, and all put into a napkin, out of which each took his piece, as out of a lottery; then each piece was broken to see what was in it, which caused much *laughter,* to see our Lieutenant prove the cuckold,

and to see us tumble over the other in the cabin, by reason of rough weather.

From the *National Mark Calendar of Cooking*. Compiled for the Ministry of Agriculture by Ambrose Heath and D.D. Cottington Taylor 1936: 'It's a pity to let old customs die out entirely, and a *"Twelfth Night Party"*, at which the cake takes pride of place, is sure to be popular. This cake was originally a highly spiced one and rather rich, but if the party was for children, a simpler mixture could be substituted. There is an opinion that outside is by far the most important. The principle decoration should be *twelve candles and stars*. A pale blue coloured icing (suggestive of a clear sky) assists in carrying out the scheme each person's ingenuity and resourcefulness can be exercised in evolving a really attractive cake worthy of the *"Feast of the Star"*

The following is a very good mixture for the recipe:

Ingredients
8oz flour

6oz currants

4 eggs

8oz sultanas

8oz sugar

2oz candied peel

8oz butter

Little milk

2oz glacé cherries

1 dessertspoonful mixed spice

Grease a cake tin and line with paper. Prepare the dry ingredients. Cream the butter and sugar together, beat each egg in separately, stir in the sieved flour and spice, fruit etc, alternately with the milk, adding a little of each at a time. Blend all the ingredients together, put into a prepared tin, and bake in a moderate oven of about 350°F for 2 hours. When cold, ice with pale blue icing (using culinary colouring) and decorate.'

Thank you so much to…

Evelyn Ainley. Sandra Beasley – for the Big Yorkshire Pud. *Fay Blackburn. Joanna Brewer* – Berry Tart recipe and 'local peculiarities'. *Fiona Brooks* for encouragement. *Susie Creane-Smith* Tannachbrae Guest House and Restaurant. Dufftown. Speyside – Lamb Shank and Tomato Consommé recipe. *Peter Charnley. Richard Davies* of Heptonstall Museum. *Ruth Dean* of Far Barsey. *Elland Reference Library. Lesley Foster* who helped hatch my fledgling concept. *Ann Fulton* for Butternut Squash Soup recipe. *Mike Grange* for his stories. *Derek Greenwood.* Halifax Reference Library. *Huddersfield Reference Library. Megan Masters. Mary Moon. Duncan Newsome* for his stories too. *Kevin Parker. Penny Perkins* for proof reading. *Matthew Royle-Evatt* Digitronix. Saddleworth Museum. *Amanda Seymour. Shirley Sidall. Nancy Smith. Paul Stevenson* Digitronix. *Keith (Irish) Taggart. Alice Thomas. Mark Travis. Nick Turley* – sheep shot and chief taster and his assistant *Betty. Hannah Warboys. Terry Warboys.* A BIG BIG thank you *Michelle Wardingley* for Testing, Home Economy and Styling and keeping me going. *Janet Whitfield. Judy Whitworth. Hillary Wood. Steve Yelland* my hero. XXX